SEEING
THROUGH
THE
DARK

SEEING THROUGH THE DARK

BLIND AND SIGHTED – A VISION SHARED

BY MALCOLM E. WEISS

Introduction by Dr. Doris E. Hadary

Illustrated with photographs

Harcourt Brace Jovanovich
New York and London

10-17-95

Printed in the United States of America

First edition

B C D E F G H I J K

Library of Congress Cataloging in Publication Data

Weiss, Malcolm E
    Seeing through the dark: blind and sighted—a
vision shared.

    Includes index.
    SUMMARY: Discusses one major problem of blind-
ness—the sighted people who fear or misunderstand
this handicap.
    1. Blind—Juvenile literature.   2. Blindness—
Juvenile literature.   3. Vision—Juvenile literature.
[1. Blind.   2. Physically handicapped]   I. Title.
HV1593.W43   362.4′1   76-17015
ISBN 0-15-272815-5

CONTENTS

ACKNOWLEDGMENTS

In writing this book, I learned much about the shared vision of blind and sighted children. My teachers included:

Sister Geraldine and her staff at the Blind Children's Resource Center, Portland, Maine;

Mrs. May B. Mongue, Itinerant Teacher of the Visually Handicapped;

The staff of the York Elementary School, York, Maine;

The faculty and staff of the Laboratory Science for the Blind Project, The American University, Washington, D.C.;

and, above all, the children themselves.

M. E. W.

INTRODUCTION

I invite you to enter my science laboratories where the sighted are working side by side with the blind. There is a feeling of excitement which prevails. Excitement in the sharing of observations, discovery, and learning.

Susan, a blind student, and Samantha, a sighted student, are partners in the laboratory. They are discussing their observations and showing each other their results in a physics experiment. I remember the first day Susan and Samantha met. Samantha held out her hand to Susan and said, "How do you do." Susan said "Hello," and turned away. Samantha looked puzzled and put down her empty extended hand. During the laboratory experiment, Samantha enthusiastically exclaimed, "Look, Susan, look at how many clips I picked up with ten turns! How many did you?" Susan held up her electromagnet and turned her head toward Samantha. However, Samantha did not really show her results to her partner in a way that she could see. Susan turned away and went back to her own activity. Samantha was puzzled and interested by the lack of response. By the end of the lesson she learned that there were many ways of seeing—she touched Susan's hand with her magnet and they both saw together, compared results, and began designing another experiment joining their batteries together. When they left the laboratory, Samantha took Susan's hand; they shook hands, embraced each other, and said, "See you next week."

Reading *Seeing Through the Dark* was for me an exciting experience of confirmation. Mr. Weiss has, with insight and art, written a book which brings the light of understanding into the realm of human interactions. He specifically relates to the blind and the sighted. However, there are greater implications and applications of his revelations for all human beings on earth. That understanding of the "why" and "how" of human behavior is essential in order that we may communicate, work, and study together, thereby enriching our lives and raising the standards of our goals.

The scientist in search of truth and knowledge is also constantly trying to find different ways of observing and expressing his observations. The scientist's world is a world of abstractions—seeing with the mind. Perhaps it is because of my long career as a scientist and teacher that I feel a great affinity for blind students who, in my laboratories, demonstrate sophistication and sensitivity in ways of observing and interpreting the world around them. Like the scientists, they observe with all their senses made possible by the nervous system and see with the mind.

Having spent several years working with blind children and blind teachers, I can, with confidence, say that exploring natural phenomena through laboratory experiences provides an important basis for the premise that understanding is the light that lets us see through the dark. This is true for both the blind and the sighted who could and should work side by side as partners in discovery and creativity.

Mr. Weiss makes these points in a manner which is never pedantic and always interesting. He has combined the knowledge of a scientist with the sensitivity of an artist to describe the ways of "seeing through the dark." It is essential in our world today that young children and adults, including school teachers and administrators, will read, transmit, and make use of his message with sensitivity and understanding.

Doris E. Hadary, Ph.D.
Professor of Chemistry and Project Director
Science Laboratory Experiences for the Blind
American University
Washington, D.C.

SEEING
THROUGH
THE
DARK

HOW MANY WAYS OF SEEING?

We all share the changes of the night. We all share pictures in the dark.

By night, a familiar bedroom can change to something strange and shadowy. You may not even see as far as its walls. You sink in sleep, perhaps to drift in dreams. Your body remains firmly anchored to the bed while your mind wanders past the invisible walls to places of memory and wishing.

But the mind must come back, and dreams must end. You may awaken so suddenly that you think you are still adrift. For a moment, the places of your dreams seem more real than the unseen room. You are lost without direction like a traveler in an unknown country.

A night light can help. You see where you are as soon as you awaken, and the wisps of dream dry up like fog in the sun. For a blind person, a clock on a bedside table does the same thing. It is a familiar noise from a familiar direction, a ticking arrow of sound pointing the way on a mental map and picture of the room.

Such pictures in the mind are not made by eyes alone. To know the shape, size, and position of something is seeing with the mind. It is what the blind girl means when she tells her friend: "I can see all right, but not with my eyes . . ."

There are many ways of seeing for all of us. We see a great deal through the sense of touch, which is why we often say of a new situation, "Well, I'm just getting the feel of it." It is not merely the artist who paints with his hands. Our fingers are like ten brushes painting on the canvas of our minds.

A cat's tongue is but a small red tongue to the eye of sight. But when a cat licks your fingers, the picture becomes unforgettable: rough as sandpaper, fluttery and damp as a breeze in a spring rain. And if the picture of the cat's tongue is at our fingertips, the portrait of the bedroom floor is in our toes: soft and warmer where the carpet is, hard and colder beyond the carpet's edge.

To you, a sunset may be a blaze of colors slowly fading against a darkening sky. It is not that to a blind person, but it is many other things as lovely. Close your eyes to the sunset and you may see them.

It is the sudden hush that comes at twilight. It is

a coolness on your face and hands that outlines the lengthening shadows. In the country, it is the silence of the birds and a freshening breeze that carries more clearly and sharply the smells of fields and woods.

Seeing does not come with light, nor darkness with the lack of sight. True darkness comes only through ignorance and misunderstanding. We understand with our minds. And understanding is the light that lets us see through the dark in as many ways as there are thoughts and feelings.

A blind scientist, Carl Weiss, may have said it best: ". . . to live is not only to see, but also to hear, to feel with the fingers as well as with the emotions, to sense, to shape, to manipulate, to converse, to think, to walk, to smell, and to taste . . ."

TO FEEL, TO SHAPE

How many buried-treasure maps have you got inside of your head?

None? Don't be too sure. You know the kind of map we're talking about: "Walk twelve paces south from the old oak tree, then five paces east. Dig!"

What kind of map is this? There's an obvious reason why the map doesn't tell us to go straight to the treasure. There's a reason why we need this map of paces and directions, where distances are measured by footsteps instead of eyes. The reason is that the treasure is buried where no eyes can see it.

You carry maps like this around inside your head all

the time. They have nothing to do with seeing. They do not depend on your eyes. They are maps of familiar places. For example, there's the map of your bedroom. Like any buried-treasure map, it is a map of paces and directions. It may use the bed for a compass: "Six paces to the right of the bed is a wall. Nine paces from the foot of the bed is a bureau." And so on.

You don't think about this map as you feel your way through a dark room. But you can tell that you're counting your steps and keeping track of which way you're moving. You're charting your movements on a map in your memory. You sense when a wall is coming up. Sometimes, you stretch out your fingers toward it. If the map is accurate, fingertips and memory meet. You feel the wall with your outstretched hands as it looms up in your memory.

Where did this map come from? How was it made?

At first thought, you might imagine the map was made from the memory of things seen many times. But that can't be the whole story. You don't count your footsteps with your eyes each time you walk through your bedroom. In fact, this map was made largely through your sense of touch.

Unlike hearing, seeing, tasting, and smelling, the sense of touch does not have a special place. You are surrounded by it, just as you are surrounded by your skin, for wherever there is skin, there is a sense of touch.

Put a postage stamp in the palm of your hand. Just beneath the skin covered by the stamp lie some six hundred nerve endings sensitive to touch. That adds up to many thousands of such nerve endings over the whole surface of the body.

These nerves help form a complete map of the skin. Like any buried-treasure map, this touch map does not depend on seeing. If someone touches you on the back, you know exactly where you have been touched. If you have an itch, you don't have to look to know where to scratch.

Sensations of touch from all over the body are transmitted to a narrow strip of the brain about one inch wide. Each spot on the skin sends its sensations to a different point in that strip. So a map of the skin is "wired" into the brain.

But the sense of touch tells us much more than *where* we are being touched. It tells us how strong the touch is: Is it a tap? A slap? A punch? And touch responds to a wide range of temperatures: Is it a cold ice cube? A cool breeze? A warm shower? A hot stove?

From these facts we paint a rich and complicated touch picture of the world around us. Most of us most of the time are not very aware of how rich this picture is. Seeing seems much more important.

But when touch is gone, it becomes a hole, a blank space right in the middle of our experience. We miss it badly.

You know this, although you have probably never thought about it. Have you ever tried walking on a foot that has "fallen asleep"? It's awkward, strange, and uncertain. Your foot seems detached from your body. You

By touch she made this picture of her best friend—a picture that can be seen with the eyes or fingertips. (*Malcolm E. Weiss*)

have to look to see where it is, but without touch it's a little hard to believe what your eyes tell you. And they tell you nothing about the feel of the floor you're trying to walk on.

Let's take a closer look at how the touch picture of the stamp in your palm got painted. As soon as the stamp touched your palm, you could feel it. The slight pressure of the stamp on your skin caused electrical and chemical changes in the nerve endings just beneath the skin. The changes flowed rapidly along the nerve, like ripples moving across a pond.

A ripple of such changes is a nerve impulse. Just as there may be many ripples traveling across a pond, so many impulses may flow along a nerve, one after the other.

A stronger pressure will usually produce a larger number of ripples crowded more closely together. This is one way in which the nerve impulses can carry information.

These impulses must reach the brain before we can become aware of them. What happens on the way?

An impulse starts, say, in a nerve cell beneath the skin. It flows along the axon, a long threadlike extension of the nerve cell. The longest axons are nerve fibers that stretch all the way from the tip of a toe to the base of the brain. But most axons are much shorter than this. Most cannot be seen without the help of a microscope.

However long or short the axon, the nerve impulse travels along it to its end. There it stops. The axon makes connections with other nerve cells, often hundreds of them. Nerve impulses reaching the end of the axon may set up new impulses in connected nerve cells. Impulses may be set up in just one connected cell, or a few, or many. How many new impulses are set up depends on how fast impulses are arriving at the connections, among other things. And how fast impulses are arriving depends on the strength of the touch or pressure that set off the original impulses.

So the pattern of impulses is changing constantly as the nature of the touch changes. These changes in pattern are just the beginning. The patterns of impulses may cross thousands of connections before they get to the brain. At each crossing new and more complex patterns may appear. Eventually, the impulses reach that inch-wide strip where the skin is mapped on the surface of the brain.

This whole process has happened in a fraction of a second, for most impulses travel faster than 100 miles an hour.

The patterns of impulses go on spreading and changing through the billions of nerve cells that make up the rest of the brain. These shifting patterns fill in the details of your touch picture of the stamp.

That may seem rather mysterious. But looked at another way, it's a matter of everyday experience.

You've been reading about how a touch picture of a stamp lying on your palm gets painted. By now, you have probably forgotten about the stamp. If you'd really been holding a stamp, you'd no longer notice it!

Why? The stamp remained still, so the pattern of

impulses produced by it did not change. There was nothing new to be learned from them. They faded out of your awareness.

In the same way, you may not notice a fly that has settled on your arm. If the fly begins to crawl, though, the crawling sensation screams for your attention.

The stamp is not going to crawl over your hand to produce a changing pattern of nerve impulses. But you can move your fingers over it and get the same result. In fact, that's the only way you can build up your touch picture of the stamp.

If you put your fingertip against the edge of the stamp and hold it there, you learn very little about what the edge is like. But when you move your fingertip over the edge, the touch picture begins to sharpen. You can feel the notched edges. Small as they are, you get some idea of their size. You can tell how stiff or how soft the paper is.

Much the same thing happens when you shift your eyes around a room to fix the details of it, or turn your head to judge the direction of a sound. And training makes both these senses keener. The crack of the bat and the arc of the ball tell the practiced outfielder how fast and how far he has to run to make a successful catch.

Touch can be strengthened by practice, too. A good machinist can feel the tension in a screw from his fingertips right through the blade of the screwdriver and can adjust the screw properly. A concert pianist knows from long experience just how hard to hit the keys to produce the sound he wants—from a whisper of notes to a thunderous chord. A sculptor imagines the statue he wishes to create. Along the nerves that control the movements of his hands, that image flows from his mind to his fingertips. Through touch his fingertips guide the tools that shape the image in the stone. A surgeon performs a delicate operation, probing tissues thinner than the thinnest paper without breaking through them. It is a job done almost entirely by feel.

Seeing by Hand

One operation, at least, has been done entirely by feel. David Hartman entered the medical school at Temple University in Philadelphia in 1972. In 1973, he performed a successful tracheotomy on a dog. He cut a narrow slit in the anesthetized animal's trachea (windpipe). Then he put a small breathing tube into the dog's windpipe.

Such operations are common in hospital emergency rooms. They can save lives when the upper part of the windpipe is blocked. Hartman's operation on the dog was just a kind of practice run—something medical students do as part of their training.

His performance was perfect. It had to be done entirely by feel because Hartman is blind.

He occasionally teases strangers by telling them he intends to be a surgeon. Actually, Hartman wants to be a psychiatrist. He came to that decision during his years in high school. He was the only blind student in his

David Hartman (*left*) became the first blind student admitted to a medical school since 1872. (*Harvey Shaman, Globe Photos, Inc.*)

home town's public school system. Both Hartman and his parents wanted him to have the experience of working, studying, and playing with people who could see, since he would have to associate with them when he grew up.

Hartman went through high school with flying colors. He was elected an officer of his class in his sophomore year and vice president of the student council as a senior. His struggles with feelings of depression and doubt made him feel closer to understanding the emotional problems of his classmates and solidified his desire to become a psychiatrist.

That goal meant preparing for medical school. It meant courses in biology. When Hartman first tried to enroll in a laboratory biology course in college, the teacher, Professor Cavaliere, thought he was crazy. But Hartman persuaded Cavaliere to let him try.

To Cavaliere's amazement, Hartman kept up with the other students. When animals were dissected, he used his hands and his sense of touch to identify organs.

Cavaliere was impressed. He got other teachers to accept Hartman in their courses. Hartman himself showed a skeptical teacher how to make special drawings of microscope views of specimens. The drawings were made up of raised dots that Hartman could "see" as he moved his fingertips over them, much as blind people read Braille—a system of raised dots corresponding to the letters of the alphabet.

Not many blind people become doctors. That is due at least in part to the fears and prejudices of sighted people. Hartman, for example, became the first blind person admitted to a medical school in a hundred years. The last one, admitted in 1872, went on to become president of the Society of Internal Medicine.

But all blind people learn to use touch to make up for their lack of sight. In a classroom, blind and sighted children are working together learning how paper is recycled. They add chemicals to the waste paper, turning it into a soft, mushy pulp. The pulp is poured over a screen and kneaded. It slowly thickens until it is strong enough to be pressed into sheets.

What's happened to the texture of the pulp? The class argues over how to describe it. Finally, Michael, a blind student who has done most of the kneading, speaks up.

"When I started kneading, it felt like oatmeal. Yuk! Now it feels like peanut butter. M-m-m-m-m!"

Michael's touch picture of the experiment has suddenly made it real and vivid for the whole class. It is an unexpected and yet familiar way of looking at a new experience.

This fully developed sense of touch enables a blind person to read Braille rapidly. The raised dots of Braille writing are about $\frac{1}{10}$ of an inch apart. A good Braille reader can scan 2,000 to 2,500 dots a minute with the fingertips, or about a hundred words a minute.

That is a part of seeing with the hands. We recognize touch as a way of seeing when we say such things as, "I'd like to see that firsthand." But more can be told by touch than the raised dots that form letters and words, or

A nearly blind student kneads pulp to make paper. At first, he tells sighted classmates, "It felt like oatmeal, but now it feels like peanut butter!" His touch picture helps classmates see the experiment in a new way. (*Malcolm E. Weiss*)

the shape and texture of objects.

Our eyes tell us when a friend is sad or happy, angry or nervous. A handshake might tell us as much, if we paid attention to it.

Olga Skorokhodova is a Russian poet who is both blind and deaf. She writes of reading the feelings of a friend in a handshake. A trembling, a stiffness in the friend's hand, the way her fingers move: all these signs tell the poet her friend is upset.

A sudden coolness on a sunlit day tells Olga Skorokhodova that a cloud is passing over the sun. But when she tries to describe this for sighted people, she writes, "I imagine the warm rays of the sun after a storm, and somewhere to the side of the sun, floating in the air a dark (to use a word that people who can see use—I only imagine it as dark), rectangular mass . . ."

She goes on to describe how the mass slowly covers the sun and cuts off its heat. She explains that she often uses the language of people who see and hear because there is no separate language for the blind and deaf.

That is true. Yet in a way, we all have the same problem. All language is limited, and we constantly have to find our way around those limits. In doing so, we speak of things we cannot see because they exist only as images in our minds.

That's what happens when we say someone is a "hard nut to crack" or an "oily personality." We are using the language of touch to describe a personality trait—and, somehow, it is more vivid than the language of sight.

It's what happens when a poem tells us more than the meaning of all its words. We might say that the poem catches a wind of meaning that blows between the words.

We can't make clear word-pictures of abstract things like moods, so we have to describe them by comparing them to familiar things combined in unlikely ways. We create pictures that exist only in our imaginations. If we say someone is green with envy, the idea seems to catch what it means to be envious. Maybe that's because green is a rather sick color for a person and envy is a sick kind of feeling.

The limits of our language, like the limits of Olga Skorokhodova's, reflect the limits of our senses.

The other senses work through the nervous system in much the same way that touch does. All sensory nerves are gadgets for translating something from the outside world—touch, taste, odor, sound, light—into nerve impulses. But there are sharp limits to the responses of these nerves.

We are all blind to the light of X-rays. Yet we have learned to use them to take pictures of broken bones. We are all deaf to the high-pitched squeaks that bats steer by in the night. Yet we have made detectors that bounce similar sounds off objects deep in the ocean so we can "see" through dark and muddy waters.

All these things—the special uses blind people make of touch, the colorful language of poetry, the discoveries and inventions of science—have much in common. They are detours around the limits of our senses. They allow us to reach our goal of understanding by other paths.

These are the paths of creative imagination; the paths of putting together familiar things in new ways. They are ways that we see through the dark.

TO HEAR, TO WALK, TO SMELL, TO TASTE

Some boys and girls crowd around the small glass tank in Dr. Doris Hadary's laboratory at the American University in Washington. The water in the tank is milky. It is full of a fine white powder, like chalk dust or starch.

Is it starch? The experimenters know of one sure way to find out. They add a tiny bit of iodine to the water —and wait. If the powder is starch, the water will turn a deep, rich blue.

"Listen," says one girl. "The color is changing!"

"It *is* starch," a boy chimes in. The others agree. They are blind youngsters taking a course in ele-

This blind girl is learning to "hear" changes in the color of light as changes in the pitch of a sound. (*Marc Moshman*)

She and a sighted classmate observe how iodine changes a colorless
solution of starch to a dark blue color. (*Marc Moshman*)

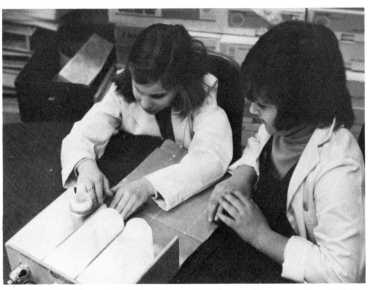
The blind girl explains her discoveries about the properties of light to her sighted friend. (*Marc Moshman*)

mentary science. As the milky water darkens to blue, they listen to it happening.

A light shines through the tank and strikes a light-sensitive cell on the other side. The light sets up a small electric current in the cell. The current, in turn, makes a buzzer sound a high-pitched whine.

As the color in the tank darkens, less light can shine through to strike the cell. The current in the cell gets weaker, and the whine of the buzzer drops in pitch.

For these boys and girls, the light-sensitive cell is a detour around their blindness. It translates the color change they cannot see into a change of pitch that they can hear.

There is a way in which these two changes are alike. Both light and sound travel in waves. The waves spread out from the source of the light or sound in all directions. In the same manner, waves spread out when you tap your finger on the still surface of a pond or a bathtub filled with water.

If you tap your finger in a steady rhythm, the waves are spaced an even distance apart. The distance between any wave and the next one is the wavelength.

If you tap your finger faster, the waves you make are closer together. You have made the wavelength shorter. If you tap your finger more slowly, the wavelength gets longer.

Light and sound can vary in wavelength, too. When the wavelength of light changes, we see different colors. Red light has the longest wavelength of any light that we can see. As the wavelengths get shorter, the color we see shifts through all the hues of the rainbow—from red through orange, yellow, green, blue, and violet.

When the wavelength of a sound changes, we hear tones of different pitch. The longest wavelengths we can hear sound like a deep, growly foghorn. As the wavelengths get shorter, the tones we hear shift through the whole range of an orchestra—from the thud of a drum to the shrill whistle of a piccolo.

So color and pitch are both due to a change in wavelength. The eye sees the change in light waves as color. The ear hears the change in sound waves as pitch.

But light waves and sound waves are different from one another in an important way. Light waves are waves of pure energy. They cannot be touched or felt as waves.

For example, light can pass through air, water, or glass. When light passes through these substances, it does not create waves in them. It does not make the air, water, or glass vibrate. The only thing that vibrates is the light itself.

But sound waves *are* vibrations of some substance— vibrations that can be *felt*. Tap a glass with a spoon to make it ring. Then touch the glass. You can feel it vibrating. Put your fingers on the sounding board of a piano that is being played. You can feel the vibrations of the sounds.

The whole surface of the body can feel sounds in this way, especially low-pitched sounds. With ears stopped, you can still feel the boom of thunder. You can feel the beat of a drum right up from the floor through your feet.

26

This ability to feel the vibrations of sound on the surface of your skin is, of course, a part of your sense of touch. And it is out of the touch sense that hearing developed.

Ears Can Touch What Hands Can't Reach

The skin is the "sense organ" of touch. As a baby grows in its mother's body, the ears develop out of the same group of cells as the skin. It is not just the outer ear —the part you can see and touch—that develops from these cells, but the inner parts as well. These are the parts that make the ear work. The shell-shaped outer ear merely helps pick up sound waves and guide them inside.

The sound waves enter the ear and move along a short passageway to the eardrum—a thin, cone-shaped piece of skin, or membrane, stretched across the passageway. The open end of the cone faces the incoming sound waves. The point of the cone touches one end of a tiny bone called the hammer.

The eardrum itself is quite small, about half the size of a dime. The sound waves make the eardrum vibrate, and the point of the cone concentrates the vibrations on the hammer.

The other end of the hammer strikes a second bone, the anvil. The anvil strikes a third bone, the stirrup.

The stirrup looks like its namesake. It is a ring with one flat side, the footplate. When the anvil strikes the opposite side, the footplate vibrates against another

27

membrane, the oval window.

The oval window rests against a sealed, fluid-filled tube. The tube is coiled like the shells of some snails, so it has been named the cochlea, from an ancient Greek word for snail.

The vibrations of the oval window send waves surging back and forth through the fluid in the cochlea. Suspended in the fluid are two more membranes, one above the other. They are covered with fine hairs. The roots of the hairs are in the lower membrane, and the hair tips are in the upper membrane.

As the sound waves race through the fluid, they make ripples in these membranes. The membranes tremble like sheets being shaken out to dry. Ripples move back and forth and sideways through them in different patterns, depending on the kinds of sound waves. The rippling membranes rock the hairs attached to them. The hairs turn the rocking motion into nerve impulses that reach your brain. And only then does hearing take place.

The whole system—from the eardrum through the three tiny bones to the oval window and the cochlea—takes up very little space. It could lie in the shell of your outer ear. The hammer anvil and stirrup are so light that 10,000 bones like them would not weigh quite half an ounce.

But the system does its job well. Part of its job is to magnify sound. The eardrum, as we have seen, is small. But it is fourteen times larger than the footplate. Yet all the sound waves picked up by the eardrum are concentrated on the much smaller area of the footplate. The sound is magnified even more in the cochlea, and it is also "taken apart." The hairs respond in different ways to different types of sound. That's why a trained conductor can listen to a hundred different instruments playing together and tell at once whether one of them is playing too fast or slow or has hit a wrong note.

As a result, the ear is incredibly sensitive. If you have good hearing, you hear fainter sounds than you are usually aware of. You can even hear the faint echoes of your footsteps bouncing off a nearby wall.

The ear is a special organ of touch that is highly sensitive to one kind of touch—the touch of sound waves. It is a kind of *touch at a distance.*

You may use touch to see with your hands quite well. But seeing with your hands is limited to what is within reach of your hands. If the cat's tongue is out of reach, it is out of sight. You can form no touch picture of it. The cat's purr, however, is within reach of your ears across the room. The mutter of thunder can be heard for miles.

The sound picture of the cat's purr can tell you more than just the fact that there is a cat nearby. It can tell you where the cat is. It can tell you whether the cat is moving, and in what direction.

The fact that you have two ears helps you to tell the direction of the sound. If the source of the sound is to the right or left, it seems louder in the corresponding ear. If the sound is directly in front of you or directly behind you, it seems equally loud in both ears.

The sound picture also has depth. If the sound is

moving away from you, it gradually becomes fainter and harder to identify, just as an object moving away from you slowly appears to become fainter and more indistinct.

Like the touch picture of your bedroom, you are rarely aware of such sound pictures. When you hear a cat behind you, you turn to look for it without thinking. It was the sound that found the cat for you. But you don't really feel you've found it until you turn around and see it. When you can see, sight seems to overwhelm and reassure the other senses.

That's the reason the teachers in the science lab do the experiments with their eyes closed. The teachers are not trying to give themselves a handicap so that they are on a level with their blind students. They are trying, in a sense, to *remove* a handicap—the handicap of sight.

"People who can see," explains Bob Haushalter, one of the lab class teachers, "use that one sense mostly. Blind people constantly use three: touch, hearing, and smell." By closing their eyes, the teachers force themselves to pay attention to what these other senses are telling them. They are raising their awareness, not lowering it.

Blind people often do this. Beth, a blind girl, is playing with one of her best friends, Steve. It's a rainy afternoon during a school holiday, and they are trading favorite records.

"Have you heard this one?" Beth says, racing across the room. Steve can see a small pile of albums right in her path. He starts to call, "Look out!" But before he can

The blind girl explores the strange feel of the fish, but the sighted girl is a little more timid about it! (*Marc Moshman*)

Together they set up another experiment with light. (*Marc Moshman*)

Instructors and students listen for the "sound" of light. (*Marc Moshman*)

make a sound, Beth nimbly jumps over the pile.

"How'd you do that?" he asks. "I thought for sure you'd trip."

"But I didn't"—she grins—"because you *did!*"

Steve is puzzled for a moment, but then he remembers. He did trip over the albums earlier. Beth heard the thump and his grunt of surprise. She added this sound picture of an obstacle to her inner map of the room. Later, she avoided the albums.

Of course, Beth didn't think all this out. She keeps track of changes in her surroundings almost automatically, just as all of us do. But she pays attention to clues that most of us ignore.

This does not mean that her other senses are better than Steve's. It just means that she has had more practice in using them. Nor does it mean that other senses can completely take the place of sight.

As one young blind girl, Judi Sorter, puts it: "I am totally blind. This means that I cannot see people, light, shadows or objects. It *does not* mean that I cannot hear, or, conversely, that I have extraordinary hearing; that I am terribly stupid or extremely bright; completely helpless or totally independent. It means that I cannot see. That my eyes do not work."

A blind girl may learn to find her own way around a strange playground. But her mental map and picture of the playground will be filled in more rapidly with the help of someone who can see. Looking is the quickest way to make a strange place more familiar.

Yet a blind person may help a sighted one fill in the

picture of a familiar place. Touch, sound, and smell are all parts of the picture, but they are the parts the sighted person does not see well.

The street noises on a city corner have a rhythm of their own that beats to the pulse of the traffic lights. Here the buses stop, doors squeaking, brakes hissing. In the middle of the block is a movie theater. Eddies of air swirl past the swinging doors: warm in winter, cool in summer, slightly stale and popcorn-laden always.

On a country road or in a city park, there is the smell of fresh-cut grass. Rain drips and taps, but snow slides softly out of the sky. The wind sings through the trees, but it sings a different song through the leaves of a maple than the needles of a pine. Birds can be recognized by their calls when they are hidden or too far away to be seen.

Teachers in schools where sighted and blind boys and girls study together sometimes take their classes on "listening and smelling" walks. At first, the sighted children do not hear or smell as much as the blind ones. Slowly the picture fills in.

A teacher wears a necklace of shells to school one day. The sighted students can see that it's unusual. But it is Jean, a blind girl, who notices the soft musical clink of the shells. Next day, the teacher wears beads. It is Jean who describes to her classmates their cool glassy feel and crisp rattle. Soon the other students begin listening as well as looking. "I want to see your necklaces, really see them the way Jean does," one says.

Sound carries other messages, too, not just from

things that make sound, but from silent places. There is the message of emptiness.

Have you ever walked through an empty house? Not just a house empty of people, but a house empty of furniture and with bare walls? A house you and your family were getting ready to move out of?

It *sounds* empty just as much as it *looks* empty. Your footsteps have a hollow ring. Your voice echoes off the walls. The echo tells you they are flat and hard.

Seeing by Ear

An echo is the reflection of sound off an object. Just as reflected light tells our eyes about an object, so reflected sound can tell our ears about it. Most of the things we see, we see by light reflected off them from a lamp, the sun, or the sky. The light reflected from the empty walls tells your eyes they are bare. The echo of your voice carries much the same information. It adds to the feeling of hollowness and emptiness.

In fact, this is a case where the sound picture is more vivid than the light picture. A house full of echoes is a lonely house.

For a blind person, echoes come to illuminate more than emptiness. The sound of footsteps fades quickly on an empty path. They bounce back sharp and clear from a brick wall, less loudly from glass, and more muffled from softer surfaces. The time the echoes take to return gives a feel of how far away obstacles are.

On dark or foggy nights, we all make some use of echoes to tell us where obstacles are. People can hear two distinct sounds about $\frac{1}{100}$ of a second apart. So you can just hear a distinct echo $\frac{1}{100}$ of a second after the original sound.

How far away is the obstacle that bounced the echo back? Sound travels through the air at about 1,100 feet a second. So in $\frac{1}{100}$ of a second, it travels 11 feet.

But that's a *round trip*. In that time, the sound has traveled to the obstacle and the echo has come back to your ears over the same path. The obstacle is about 5½ feet away.

Actually, we can detect obstacles by their echoes at much shorter distances. The echo is usually different from the original sound, and we can hear that difference even when sound and echo overlap.

A blind person must depend more completely on sounds. He may learn to use echoes to tell him where an obstacle is, how far away it is, how big it is, and whether it is made of hard or soft materials.

To develop this ability takes lots of practice. Wearing metal plates on the heels or whistling or clapping while walking helps develop this skill. All these things make rather high-pitched sounds. And high-pitched sounds reflect better from smaller objects. Their echoes give a better image of such objects.

That's because these sounds have a short wavelength. The sounds we hear most often—sounds in the range of the human voice or the middle notes on a piano —have waves that are spaced several feet apart. Such

37

waves go around small obstacles without being reflected at all. But the sound waves produced by clapping or the tap of metal heels or whistling are just a fraction of an inch apart.

If *you* try to make use of echoes in this way, you must think about what you're doing. Someone blind from birth has had long practice in using echoes. He doesn't need to think about using them. He just feels the echoes directly as awareness of the obstacle. His hearing obstacles is as direct an experience as your seeing them.

Responding to a friend's questions about how he went about camping, David Hartman remarked: "I don't experience anything different. It's just that I hear things instead of see things. So big deal!"

Actually, you went through the same sort of hard practice to learn how to see—to understand the meaning of what your eyes show your brain. But you did all your practicing when you were so young that you don't re member it.

For example, you can tell the difference between a ball and a cube at a glance. But that's the result of prac tice. One proof is what happens when someone who has been blind from birth becomes able to see later on. He can tell the difference between a ball and a cube easily— by closing his eyes and feeling it! He can't tell the differ ence by looking until he has had experience. And it takes weeks of experience for him to learn to judge the size and distance of things by sight.

What he sees at first is just a confusing jumble of light, shadow, and color. Gradually, through experience,

A partially sighted student uses touch to study his monarch butterfly caterpillars (in the jar) and tells his friends about it. (*Malcolm E. Weiss*)

his mind draws meaning out of the jumble. Objects, sizes, and shapes are sorted out of the confusion.

You experience the same sort of confusion at first if you try to hear obstacles. With practice, the confusion is sorted out.

Hearing and seeing are two different ways of understanding what's around us. Yet we say, "I see," when what we mean is, "I understand," because we usually understand what we see. We only half understand what we hear. And it is understanding that counts. It takes the mind to make sense out of the senses.

TO THINK, TO SENSE —THE MIND'S EYE

A horseshoe bat flies through the dark air squeaking. Its squeaks are much too high-pitched for a human ear to hear. And if they could be heard, they would sound not like separate squeaks but one long whistle of sound. The bat squeaks some one hundred times a second.

The bat stops its ears to its own squeaking. As it squeaks, it tightens muscles to prevent the tiny bones within its ears from vibrating. Between each squeak, the muscles relax briefly. The bat listens. It listens for the size, shape, and distance of obstacles, danger, and food.

The horseshoe bat gets its name from two horseshoe-shaped folds of skin around its nose. These folds, like the cup-shaped fold of skin that is your outer ear, are used to aim sounds. The outer ear, however, aims sounds *into* your ear. The horseshoe bat uses its "horseshoe" to aim pulses of sound *out* from its nose.

By moving the folds from side to side, the bat aims a narrow beam of sound in different directions, like a flashlight lighting up the dark. The beam makes echo pictures of what's around the bat. The longer the time between squeak and echo, the farther away is the object causing the echo. If the quality of the echo changes suddenly, the bat's sound beam has crossed an edge or corner of the object.

The bat's echo pictures show very small objects clearly. That's because the wavelength of the bat's cries is about $\frac{1}{10}$ of an inch. As a rough rule, sounds of a given wavelength will not form a clear echo picture of objects much smaller than the wavelength. Thus, middle C on the piano has a wavelength of a little over four feet. Middle C will not form clear echo pictures of anything much smaller than that.

On the other hand, the bat's echo picture of a gnat a mere $\frac{1}{25}$ of an inch across is quite sharp. That's helpful to the bat since gnats and mosquitoes are among its favorite foods.

So the idea of bats lighting up the dark with sound is more than a figure of speech. The horseshoe bat can catch gnats that appear like mere dots to us, and dodge around fine wires in the dark—wires barely visible to us in broad daylight.

Of course, we can't hear the kinds of sounds that

bats make to steer and find food by. Nor can we make pictures of objects using the echoes of such sounds . . .

Neither of those statements is quite true. In some hospitals, doctors are doing both.

A one-year-old girl falls on a slippery floor and strikes her head. Her mother comforts her, and the child seems all right. But a few hours later, she is dizzy and sick. Frightened, the mother calls a doctor and rushes the child to the hospital.

The doctor holds something that looks like a penlight to the side of the baby's head. Wires connect the "penlight" to an instrument panel with many dials and a screen that resembles the screen on a TV set.

In fact, the screen works exactly the way a TV screen works. No light comes from the "penlight," and the examining room is still. But as mother and doctor watch, three parallel lines of light blaze up on the screen.

The lines on either side are echo pictures of the sides of the girl's head. The line between them is an echo picture of the midline of the girl's brain.

The brain is divided into right and left halves. Only a narrow bridge of nerve bundles connects them. The midline echo of the child's brain should be just halfway between the echoes marking the sides of her head.

It is not. It is shifted to the right. This can only mean that something is pushing her brain to one side. Probably, when she fell, a blood vessel was injured on the left side of her head. Blood oozing from the vessel and trapped in her skull is pressing her brain toward the right.

The trouble has been located quickly, and that is important. The pressure might soon cause permanent brain damage. But now the excess blood is drained off before any damage results. The blood vessel heals, and the baby is back to normal.

Scenes like this one are not unusual in hospitals nowadays. Like a bat, the penlight-shaped instrument sends out short rapid pulses of extremely high-pitched sound. As we've seen, these sounds are far above the range of human hearing, so they are called "ultrasound," from the Latin word "ultra," meaning "above."

The "penlight" is really an ultrasonic probe. When it sends out a pulse of ultrasound, it is acting like a loudspeaker. Between each pulse it becomes an extremely sensitive microphone. It "listens" for the returning echo.

The probe changes the sound of the echo into electrical signals. These signals are fed into a computer. The computer measures the time between each pulse and its returning echo.

Using this information, the computer sends the signals to different parts of the screen. There, the electrical signals are converted into light. The screen forms a visible image of the probe's echo pictures.

Ultrasound probes, in the words of one scientist, "put the doctor's eyes inside the patient." A doctor can watch echo pictures of the heart at work. He can even watch the blood circulating inside the heart and see the heart valves open and close. A surgeon can locate damage to organs deep in the body *before* he begins to operate.

And ultrasound can reach deep into the metal parts

of an airplane engine. It can light up cracks and weaknesses in the metal before the engine is put into use.

The ultrasound probe is much like the light-sensitive cell that blind children use in the Washington science lab. Both do the same sort of job. The light-sensitive cell turns light the children cannot see into sounds that they can hear. The probe turns sounds we cannot hear into images that we can see.

More important, both instruments relate *changes* that we are not aware of to *changes* that we can sense. The changes we can sense then become a mind's-eye image of changes beyond our senses. The light-sensitive cell relates changes in brightness to changes in pitch. The probe relates changes in a sound echo to changes in an image on a screen. The changes in the echo depend on the difference in the objects reflecting the echo. So the image on the screen becomes an image of these objects.

Our sense organs do the same thing. They relate changing patterns of light or sound, for example, into changing patterns of nerve impulses. Man-made instruments that do a similar job are called transducers. They are often like extensions of our senses, allowing us to hear the inaudible and see the invisible. And their invention came about largely through the search for "invisible light."

Past the Ends of the Rainbow

To study kinds of light that can't be seen, scientists must make use of transducers. In just the same way, blind children can study how visible light works. Though it is "invisible" for them, they can learn about brightness, color, heating effects, and other properties of light.

It was Sir William Herschel, a British astronomer, who first used the phrase "invisible light." Herschel wanted to find out which part of the sun's light carried the most heat. He knew that sunlight is a mixture of many different wavelengths or colors. When sunlight is passed through a prism, the path of the rays is bent. The red rays, of longest wavelength, are bent least. The violet rays, of shortest wavelength, are bent most. So the different wavelengths are spread out and separated as they pass through the prism. They appear as a rainbow of colors from red through violet. This regular arrangement of colors according to change in wavelength is a spectrum.

Which rays in the spectrum carry the most heat? In 1799, Herschel tried an experiment to find the answer. He passed sunlight through a prism, forming a spectrum. Then he moved a thermometer through the different colored bands in the spectrum. As Herschel moved the thermometer from violet toward the red end of the spectrum, the temperature got warmer.

Herschel reached the red edge of the spectrum. He moved the thermometer *beyond* the edge—and it got warmer still!

As a result, Herschel decided that there was light beyond the red end of the spectrum, where no light could be seen. Since the spectrum is an orderly sequence of wavelengths, this light must have a longer wavelength than red. Today, these invisible rays are known as heat rays or infrared, from the Latin "infra," below. Infrared rays carry much of the heat from the sun and other hot objects to us.

We can't see infrared, but we can feel its heating effects. It is this light that Olga Skorokhodova felt shaded from when a cloud passed over the sun. It is this light we feel when we hold a hand near a light bulb that's just been turned off and is still hot.

Other experiments soon showed that there is light beyond the violet end of the spectrum, too. This light is shorter in wavelength than violet and is called ultraviolet. Though it is also invisible, we notice some of its effects. It can expose photographic film. It can cause a tan or a sunburn.

There is light beyond the ends of the rainbow. Like visible light, infrared and ultraviolet are waves of pure energy. And in the 1860s, another British scientist, James Clerk Maxwell, created a theory about such waves. The theory predicted that other forms of "invisible light" existed. Though not visible, they would behave like visible light in other ways. For example, they would travel at the same speed—186,000 miles a second. And they could be reflected.

In fact, these waves would be just like visible light waves in every way—except wavelength. Our eyes are only sensitive to a small portion of these waves.

How small a portion? Think back a moment to the way a prism spreads out sunlight into all the colors of the rainbow. The spectrum is something like a piano keyboard. On a keyboard, the musical notes are arranged in regular order, from the longest wavelength to the shortest. In the spectrum the colors are arranged in order of wavelength.

There is a way that we can compare the size of the piano keyboard to the size of the color keyboard. We can use the change in wavelength as a measuring rod. If we start counting with middle C on the piano and count up eight white keys, we come to another C. This C is an octave above middle C. Every time we go up an octave, we come to a note that has half the wavelength of the note we started from. Thus, middle C has a wavelength of about 52 inches, and the C an octave above has a wavelength of about 26 inches.

A piano keyboard is about seven octaves long. But the entire stretch of visible light—the color keyboard—is barely one octave in length. The red at one end of the rainbow is just about twice the wavelength of the violet at the other end. These wavelengths are very short compared to those of sound, but they can be measured. Red is about $\frac{1}{33,000}$ of an inch. Violet is about $\frac{1}{66,000}$ of an inch.

Maxwell's theory implied that the spectrum stretched far beyond its visible ends. There are waves still longer than infrared and waves still shorter than ultraviolet. We are unaware of them. But they are there, and they are waves of the same kinds of energy as the waves of the light we can see.

What kinds of energy? Maxwell wrote that all these waves, including visible light, are made up of electrical and magnetic energy.

Maxwell's fellow scientists knew that electricity and

magnetism are closely related. You can prove this relationship to yourself with a magnetic compass, a dry cell, and a couple of feet of bell wire. Hook up one end of the wire to a dry cell terminal. Place the wire over the compass parallel to the needle. Touch the free end of the wire *briefly* to the other terminal. Don't keep it there or you'll quickly drain all the power out of the cell.

As soon as a current flows through the wire, the needle jumps. The current has created a magnetic force around the wire. The force moves the needle. And the reverse is also true. If a coil of wire moves through a magnetic field, an electric force is generated that causes a current to flow through the wire. The electric generators in powerhouses work in this way.

All these ideas were familiar and acceptable to Maxwell's contemporaries. But that light was made up of what Maxwell called electromagnetic waves was much harder for them to get used to. Could light have anything in common with electricity and magnetism? Where was the evidence?

You may have noticed one such piece of evidence in the last chapter—the light-sensitive cell. The working part of such a cell is usually a very thin sheet of metal. When light strikes the metal, it sets up an electrical current in it.

But light-sensitive cells were unknown when Maxwell created his theory of electromagnetic waves. To many scientists of his time, Maxwell's ideas were beautiful theories that could not be put to the test, especially his prediction about other kinds of electromagnetic waves.

Some thirty years later, scientists were still looking for evidence that these waves existed. One scientist, a German named Heinrich Hertz, was producing a series of powerful electric sparks in his laboratory. The sparks jumped across a gap between two metal rods and caused an electric current to surge back and forth across the rods.

According to Maxwell's theory, this surge of current would produce a changing magnetic force around the gap. The magnetic force, in turn, would produce a changing electric force, and so on. These forces would spread out in ripples or waves of electromagnetic energy from their source at the spark.

But how to detect these waves? Hertz had built a wire hoop with a gap in it where a spark could form. This hoop was not connected to the metal rods in any way. But, Hertz reasoned, suppose the waves existed. Then they would set up an electric current in the hoop. And under the right circumstances, the current would be strong enough to cause sparks to jump across this second gap.

Sparks crackled from the rods. Hertz walked around the room carrying his hoop, and at certain spots in the room, sparks flashed between the ends of the hoop! What's more, Hertz realized that these spots were places where *reflection* from the room's walls would concentrate the waves.

Hertz wrote, describing his experiments: "We have applied the term rays of electric force to the phenomena which we have investigated. We may perhaps further call them rays of light of very great wavelength. The experiments . . . remove any doubt as to the identity of light, radiant heat, and electromagnetic wave action."

Within two years, Hertz was able to make still more convincing experiments. He showed that a sheet of flat metal would reflect the waves just as a flat mirror reflects light waves. He showed that a sheet of curved metal would concentrate the waves at a point, just as a curved magnifying mirror will concentrate visible light.

These experiments were only a beginning. Hertz's hoop was a crude sort of wave detector that reacted to the waves by making a spark. It was like a crudely designed eye that can barely tell the difference between light and dark. It was a transducer. The original spark produced electromagnetic waves. The hoop converted the waves back into sparks.

As time went on, more and more sensitive transducers were built. All of them converted one kind of changing energy pattern into another.

Some could pick up the human voice or the sound of music and translate them into patterns of electromagnetic waves. The waves could be transmitted thousands of miles and picked up by other transducers that would convert them back to voice or music again.

Today, of course, the waves that Maxwell predicted and Hertz discovered are called radio waves. They carry sounds and television images around the world. From TV cameras aboard spacecraft, they bring us close-up views of other planets. And radio waves have allowed us to detect stars that we cannot see at all.

The light from these stars is hidden behind huge

clouds of dust in space. But, like all very hot objects, the stars also give off radio waves. These waves pass through the dust clouds and reach the earth.

Radio waves are, as Hertz said, much longer than waves of visible light. Some are over a mile long. The shortest, used in radar, are about ½ inch long. Since radar bounces radio waves off objects to detect them, this small wavelength is important.

Radio waves lie below the infrared end of the spectrum. Just as man discovered ways to detect radio waves, so he discovered that there is light far beyond the ultraviolet end of the spectrum. Today, the known length of what Maxwell called the electromagnetic spectrum is about 70 octaves—ten times the range of a piano keyboard. And of all that range, only one octave in the middle is visible to human eyes. The rest, as far as our senses go, might not exist.

But it does exist. Maxwell saw its existence in his mind's eye. Hertz began the job of extending our senses to awareness of these invisible waves.

As our awareness extended, we began to see the world in different ways. The waves first seen with the mind's eye gave new visions to the eye of sight.

X-rays, for example, which lie above the ultraviolet, show us the bones beneath the skin. With X-rays we may see a man as a walking skeleton, the muscles and other organs just a filmy cloud around his moving bones.

This is a view of man quite useful to the doctor. Even for a doctor, however, this view has its limits. Muscles and soft tissues hardly exist. X-rays pass through

RADIO WAVES   MICROWAVES   INFRAR

All visible light is only a narrow part of the electromagnetic spectrum, pictured above. On the outer edges of the spectrum, radio, micro, and gamma waves bring us images of stars and galaxies invisible to the unaided eye. In the drawing at far left, infrared, or heat rays, make the warm places appear bright and the cool places dark. The next drawing shows the familiar world seen by visible

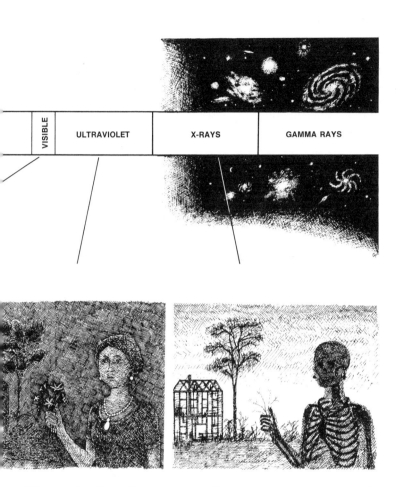

light. In the third drawing, ultraviolet is reflected in the woman's jewelry and lines in the flowers (which bees can see, even though people cannot). Seen by X-rays in the drawing on the far right, the house becomes a framework of metal parts and the woman a framework of bones. (*Gary Tong*)

them almost as if they weren't there.

The same skills and knowledge that make us able to see by means of X-rays now enable us to see by means of ultrasound. That gives us still another view of man—a view between the outer skin and the inner bones, a view of the working organs of the body.

In the beginning, this view was not an image on a screen. It was a confusion of sounds and echoes brought to us by our newly invented sense organs. To sort it out, we had to understand. We had to understand how ultrasound is affected as it bounced off different kinds of tissues. We had to find out what the echoes were telling us. Only then did the echo become a picture.

TWO WAYS OF SEEING

Thought and imagination have stretched our senses. They have given us new views of the world.

But with our unaided eyes, we can also view the world in two quite different ways. That's because we have two different sets of eyes.

Only one of these views is really familiar to us—the view of the light-filled world of daytime. We work, think, and play by the light of the sun. When night falls, we flip a switch and flood the dark with light of our own making.

It is not until we are ready to sleep that we douse the lights and let night in. And then we soon close our eyes to it.

If we awake, we turn the lights back on. Or we rely, for once, on other senses. We listen. We use our hands and perhaps our noses. We do not think about what we see in the dark, so we fail to see that with our night eyes the world is changed.

On one dark, moonless night, however, a man went walking in his garden. It was hot, and Jan Purkinje could not sleep.

It was hard to see by starlight. But Purkinje could feel the open petals of the poppies with his fingers. He could tell some of the flowers apart by their smell.

When he thought about it, Purkinje realized that he could see fairly well. It was not so much that it was hard to see as that what he was seeing was *different*. It was the difference that made him rely more on his hands and his nose than on his eyes.

There was no color in the garden, just shades of gray. The blue irises were a bright patch of gray, the yellow primroses darker. The orange poppies, bright in the sun, were now nearly black and invisible.

The garden was the same garden that he knew so well by day. But what was bright by day seemed dim by night. What seemed dark in the sunlight was bright beneath the stars. Had his eyes changed?

That we cannot see colors in dim light has probably been known for many centuries. It must have been common knowledge when there was nothing to light the night but the moon or an occasional fire. The knowledge was passed on in sayings such as "When all candles be out, all cats be gray."

But Purkinje, a Czech scientist, was one of the first to wonder why sight by night is different from sight by day. He asked himself: What kinds of light seem brightest to us? Is there only one answer to the question? Or does the way we see brightness change from day to night?

To find out, Purkinje let a beam of sunlight pass through a prism. In the shuttered laboratory, the beam was a sharp stab of light. It spread to a rainbow, glowing on the wall.

Purkinje could see that the brightest part of the spectrum was in the yellow-green. He made the sunbeam more narrow and more dim. The strip of colored lights upon the wall faded too until, in the darkening room, he could no longer see it.

Purkinje waited. His eyes got used to the dark, and he could see the strip again, but now it was gray. Parts of the strip were clearly brighter than other parts. He marked the brightest place with a pencil.

Then he widened the sunbeam once more. As the light grew stronger, color returned to the spectrum. The pencil mark was bathed in blue-green light.

It was nearly twenty-five years since Herschel had moved a thermometer through the spectrum. Herschel had asked, "What is the warmest part of the spectrum?" and the answer led him to invisible light.

Purkinje asked, "What is the brightest part of the spectrum?" and the answer was: It depends. Our eyes have two ways of seeing.

Seeing begins with light. Light comes into our eyes through a transparent outer coating, the cornea. From

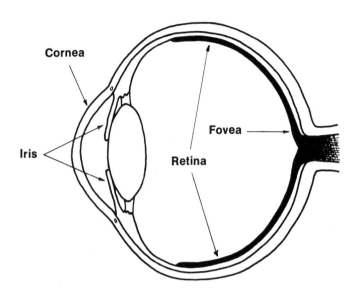

A cross section of the human eye. (*Gary Tong*)

there, light travels through the central hole in a dough-nut-shaped ring of muscle called the iris. The iris can shrink and expand to control the amount of light getting into the eye. The pupil is nothing more than the hole in the doughnut, a kind of porthole opening into the eye.

In dim light, the iris opens the porthole wide. In bright light, the iris closes the porthole down to pinhole size. That stops too much light from getting into the eye and damaging it.

After entering the pupil, the light rays pass through the lens. The lens bends the rays so that they form an image at the back of the eye. In much the same way, a

58

magnifying glass will form a small upside-down image of a bright lamp on a wall.

At the back of the eye lies the retina—a mass of tissue about the size of a postage stamp and not much thicker. The retina is the screen on which the image falls. But the retina is more than a screen. It reacts to the image projected onto it by the lens.

The retina is made up of two kinds of light-sensitive cells, the rods and the cones. The cells react to light by sending nerve impulses to the brain. The cones produce sensations of color. They are most sensitive to yellow-green light.

The rods "report" only shades of gray, like a black-and-white film. Black-and-white film is more sensitive to some colors than others. These colors appear as brighter shades of gray in photographs. The same kind of thing is true of the rods. They are most sensitive to blue-green light.

There's another important difference between rods and cones. Each cone cell sends its message to the brain along a single nerve fiber. The message is clear and unmixed with messages from other cone cells.

But large groups of rods all share the same nerve fiber. So the messages from a number of rods must travel along the same fiber. They are mixed together and will not be as clear.

For this reason, you cannot see fine details as clearly with the rods as with the cones. Suppose, for example, that you keep your eyes fixed on one word on this page. You may be able to read one or two other words while doing this, but that's all. The rest of the page is too fuzzy to read. You can't see small details well enough to tell one letter from another.

When you stare directly at the word, its image falls on a tiny area at the center of the retina—an area no bigger than the period ending this sentence. This tiny area, the fovea, is packed with some 15,000 cone cells that let you see each letter in the word clearly. The image of the surrounding words does not fall on the fovea, but more toward the edge of the retina. Just around the fovea, there are fewer cones and many rods. The cones thin out toward the retina's edge, until near the edge there are only rods.

That's why you see something more clearly when you look straight at it. The farther an object is from the center of your vision, the farther is its image from the center of your retina—and the more indistinct it appears.

But that is only true of daytime seeing. In daylight, or under bright lights at night, we are seeing primarily with the help of the cones. We can see colors and small details in objects.

But in dim light, the cones stop working. We see with the rods. The cones work very well in daylight. The rods work very well in light a billion times more dim. They enable you to see the flame of a candle miles away on a dark night. They allow you to pick a path around stones and fallen branches by the light of the stars.

Our retinas have large numbers of both rods and cones. There are about 120,000,000 rods and 7,000,000 cones in the retina of each eye. This mixture of rods and cones gives us, in effect, two sets of eyes—and two worlds of seeing. There is the familiar world of day. And there is the night world that we are rarely aware of.

It is a world we might share with many animals. Many animals are nocturnal. They are active by night. From the barn owl hunting over snowy fields to the insect-eating gecko lizard of tropical jungles, these animals spend their waking hours in the gray, shadowy night world.

It is a world of darkness, but never of complete dark. Human eyes can see by the faint glow of starlight. The retinas of many nocturnal animals have only rods, and they can see by light a thousand times dimmer than this. Their eyes are especially sensitive to motion, to changes in the patterns of dim and shadowy light.

You can share the experience of seeing in this way. There is a part of your eye that is especially sensitive to motion. In fact, it is sensitive *only* to motion.

Stare straight ahead and fix your eyes on some small object. Put one hand behind a side of your head so that you can't see it. Move your hand slowly forward, with your forefinger sticking out and wagging. As soon as you glimpse the finger out of the corner of your eye (remember to keep your eyes looking straight ahead), stop wagging it. The finger vanishes from sight. Wag it again, and it reappears.

The image of the finger falls on the extreme edge of your retina. Here, there are only rods, and they are very thinned out. They react only to a moving object. This is why a sudden motion or a change of scene at the corner

Large eyes help, but owls can track down mice in total darkness by listening to the sound of their footsteps. (*New York Zoological Society photo*)

of your eye attracts your attention.

But you can share the world of darkness more completely than this—in a darkened bedroom by night, in a movie theater, or in a starlit moonless country field. For example, when you first turn out the light in your bedroom, the room looks quite dark. You can see very little. Gradually, you see more and more. The room seems to be getting brighter.

But of course it isn't. You are simply changing from your "day eyes" to your "night eyes."

The way this change happens explains why the room seems to get brighter. First, the irises of your eyes open up to let in as much light as possible, so more of what light there is actually enters your eyes. Second, the rods slowly become more active while the cones "shut down," so your eyes are getting more sensitive to dim light. After about half an hour to forty-five minutes, you are seeing with the help of your rods alone. You have put on your "night eyes."

There are no colors, only shades of gray. Blues and greens are bright gray. Oranges and reds are almost black.

This is one proof that your night eyes use only the rod cells. Another is that you can't see fine details. You can see the print on this page by starlight as lines of black across a white page. But you can't make out the shapes of the letters.

What about the tiny area at the center of the retina, the fovea? If it is made up entirely of cones and if cones don't work in dim light, there should be a tiny blind spot right at the center of our vision.

There is. The best way *not* to see something in dim light is to stare straight at it. Stargazers know this quite well. If you look straight at a very dim star—one you can barely see—it will disappear. Look a bit to one side of it, and it pops up again.

Country people know this trick for seeing by starlight too. Is that a dark rock ahead or a small hole in the ground? Look around it, not at it, and your night eyes will find out.

By daytime standards, the world of night seeing is topsy-turvy. It is as if the rules of seeing by day were magically reversed. Colors are gray. Dark is bright, and bright dark. Outlines are fuzzy. The best way to see something is to look away from it.

But it is not magic, and it is not the world that changes. The world is so rich that our senses at their best only perceive part of it. Our night eyes give us a rare second chance to perceive it in a new way without outside help.

If the way is sometimes dim and shadowy, the other senses we have almost forgotten are sharpened. We feel for the familiar path beneath our feet. We hear the sound of a brook or the whistle of wind around a familiar corner fade with distance. The smells of a garden grow stronger as we approach it.

And we think, perhaps, of how much we know in the mind's eye alone—the swirl of planets and stars invisible in the night; the thoughts behind the smile of a friend; the whole world of memory.

SEEING
THROUGH
THE
DARK

Night is a time of things dimly seen, of things that vanish when you look straight at them. We glimpse a darting shadow out of the corner of our eye; when we turn to look, there seems to be nothing there.

The tricks and uncertainties of night seeing are one reason why ghosts and goblins come out only after dark. They cannot exist in the hard, clear bright world of day, where objects are solid and shadows are empty. Too often it seems the other way around at night.

So we shut our eyes to the night. We become blind to the night and do our seeing by day.

Of course, we don't think of that as being blind.

Being blind means living in a world where there is *no* day, where everything is always dark and hidden. It means being helpless, lonely, separated from those we love. It means being bewildered and ignorant.

That's the way we often think of blindness. And when we say, "I'm completely in the dark," we mean some or all of those things.

Many parents of blind children have feelings like this too, especially when their children are still very young. They are terrified of accidents. They are afraid to let the children walk, jump, and explore, even inside the house.

These fears usually vanish when the parents see the child in a nursery school playing and learning with other children. Like all young children, they have a lively curiosity. And there are many ways for them to satisfy it.

They may play for a while in a tunnel made of cardboard or metal. They can tell what it's made of by the change in the sound of their footsteps as they walk into it. A boy stands on tiptoe, feeling his head touch the tunnel top and getting an idea of how tall he is.

A girl lets a balloon with pellets in it float up to the ceiling. When it hits, she can hear the pellets rattle—a sound picture of how high the room is. The blind children learn to do with their other senses much of what the sighted children do with their eyes. In a mixed classroom, a blind child will often notice when a stranger comes into the room before her friends who can see do.

After a few days of nursery school, the parents' feelings about a blind child may change completely. One mother said, "I wouldn't have even tried to teach Beth to feed herself. I didn't think she could climb a slide or ride a kiddie car. Now I know she has to have her falls and learn to get around just like anyone else. She's not 'that poor blind child.' She's herself, and she's going to make it."

It was not Beth who had changed, but her mother. Her mother had been dressing Beth in her own fears and bad feelings about blindness. Those feelings had nothing to do with the way Beth felt.

Beth, in fact, has plenty of self-assurance. One day, running through her backyard in great excitement, she slammed into the big maple tree.

Beth knew perfectly well the tree was there. She knows where everything in the yard is. But in her excitement over the arrival of a friend, she had forgotten.

Her mother was not too sympathetic. "You know that tree's right in the middle of the yard," she said. "If you don't remember to watch out for it, what do you expect me to do about it?"

"Move it!" snapped Beth.

But this was long after Beth's mother had gotten over her fears. Those of us who can see often make the same mistake about blind people that she did. We never see a blind person as he or she is, but rather as our fears about blindness make them appear to us. We are afraid of being blind. We are afraid of being in the dark. We think we know that blindness is a terrible and hopeless condition in which to live. But we do not see that these are *our* fears. What we see, or think we see, is that this is the way the blind person feels. We do not, in fact, see another person, but a scarecrow dressed in the odd rags and tatters of our fears. What we see is not really there. We make ourselves blind to the blind.

Seeing Ideas

It is easiest to see this attitude in the parents of very young children. The parents can express their own feelings because they know what they are. But it is very hard to know exactly what a baby is feeling, or exactly what it wants, until the baby learns how to talk. You can tell whether a baby is happy or unhappy, hungry or tired, by looking and listening. But does the baby want a doll, a toy, a piece of apple, or a banana? Without words all the looking and listening in the world won't help; you just have to guess. This is especially true of a blind baby who can't see or point to things around him.

What's missing is the one thing that all people have in common: language. Language is the one way we have of seeing into someone else's mind. It is the one way that we can see with our mind's eye something of what another person is seeing. Words are ideas made visible.

They are not visible to the eye alone. They can be heard or they can be read. They can be read by the eyes as print or by the fingertips as raised dots on a page. They can be spoken by the tongue or by the sign language of the deaf or tapped out on the palm.

Language might be called the organ of a sixth sense

A girl reading Braille. Her fingers scan the pattern of raised dots like eyes scanning a line of print. (*Malcolm E. Weiss*)

Learning to type Braille on a special typewriter. (*Malcolm E. Weiss*)

The girl in the dark sweater is blind. But the stories she writes in Braille draw vivid pictures of her friends. (*Malcolm E. Weiss*)

—the sense of understanding. It is a most important part of being human. When Helen Keller felt and understood for the first time the word "water," she began to live and think as a complete human being.

In spite of the old saying that a picture is worth a thousand words, language is usually more important to understanding than seeing. Few of us know what it's like to be in an earthquake or to pitch a no-hitter. A movie—complete with sound—might give us some small idea. But a few well-chosen words from the victim or the pitcher can be worth lots of pictures.

The same is true of the experience of being blind. What blind people say about themselves can help us see them.

Judi Sorter knows that she can expect to meet some sighted people nearly every day who do not see her as a person living and enjoying her own life. She writes: "I have problems, but so do you. I have learned to deal with my problems, as well as I can, just as everyone should. I want you to understand that I'm not so different really."

Of course, one of blind people's main problems is the up-tight attitude of some sighted people. David Hartman's weapon against it is humor. Once at a party he was being pestered by a girl who could think of nothing to talk about but the fact that he was blind. She couldn't believe that he could be both blind and a medical student.

Hartman tried being polite and cool. But when she finally asked him point-blank whether he was really blind, Hartman's sense of whimsy got the better of him.

He reassured her that he wasn't always blind. When he drank beer, his sight came back. The girl was open-mouthed. Hartman took a final swig out of the beer can he was holding and tossed it away. It plunked into a wastebasket. To Hartman, the sound was not a plunk, but more like a perfect squelch.

Now Hartman had a pretty good idea where the wastebasket was, so it was not entirely luck that he hit it. And Hartman's sense of humor is not at all due to luck. It is because he can see himself as he really is that he can make jokes about his blindness. Like Judi Sorter, he knows that he has problems—but so do we all.

But though Hartman sees himself clearly, some sighted people do not. It doesn't help to walk up to them and say, "Look, the only thing that's different about me is that my eyes don't work." That's all they can think about anyway. Nor does it help to say, "I have problems, but so do you." They don't want to hear about *their* problems.

Hartman's way around the problem is the joke. The joke is partly on himself and partly on the narrow, squint-eyed vision of people who think they're seeing clearly. It's hard to be serious and solemn and sorry for someone who can laugh at his own limitations—and yours.

And you can't feel sorry for someone who shares her gifts and talents with you. Lisa is a fifth-grader in public school in York, Maine. She is going blind. She can still see, but just barely and not well enough to read or write, so she has learned to read Braille and use a Braille type-writer.

She uses the typewriter a lot because Lisa loves to

write stories about herself and her classmates. Most of them have normal sight and can't read Braille. But that doesn't matter. Every morning, Lisa brings in her newest batch of stories and reads them to the class. For them, Lisa is *the* storyteller. They have come to know her through sharing her stories, as Hartman's friends share his humor.

Seeing Each Other

Language is the pathway of most human sharing. And it is a pathway that babies lack. That is one reason why blind babies are usually slower to learn than sighted ones. They don't see objects. You can't use words to tell them about objects.

By taking a hint from the bats, a Scottish scientist has invented a gadget to help blind babies see with ultrasound. It is a transducer about the size of a half dollar that is strapped to the baby's forehead. It sends out pulses of ultrasound. The echoes are changed into sounds the baby can hear through earphones.

The closer an object is, the lower the pitch of the sound gets. The bigger it is, the louder the sound. Hard objects make sharp echoes, soft objects fuzzy ones. And just as with ordinary hearing, an object to one side of the baby produces a louder echo in that ear.

One baby, a boy named Dennis, learned to use the gadget well in a few months and became much more alert to his surroundings. He can easily recognize his mother and his best-loved toy—a wooden caterpillar—by their echo pictures.

This device might be used to help older blind children and adults as well. Other scientists are working on an instrument that may help blind people see in a more direct way.

The instrument depends on the fact that when any part of the visual center in the brain is stimulated, a person sees a flash of light. This is why you may "see stars" when you are hit on the head. Blind people as well as sighted people can see such flashes of light, which are called phosphenes.

Phosphenes seem to appear in different positions in space, depending on which point in the visual center is stimulated. A group of phosphenes can be made to form a pattern of light flashes. And this is the idea behind the instrument.

The instrument uses a device like a TV camera to form an image of something. Points of the image are translated into electrical signals that are sent to different parts of the visual center, producing phosphenes. The pattern of the phosphenes reproduces the pattern of the camera image, and the person sees this pattern.

So far, only rather crude versions of such an instrument have been made. They have been tried on a few blind volunteers, and they have worked to some extent. The volunteers were able to see simple patterns, including letters.

Whether such an instrument can be developed to the point where it will really be useful for blind people is still very uncertain. But Dr. Herbert Schimmel, one of the pioneers in this research, points out that the possibility of such devices raises other questions.

If they are perfected, Dr. Schimmel asks, "Will it be permissible for a blind person to be a non-user?"

Dr. Schimmel has good cause for raising such a question. A few years ago, he attended a conference on artificial visual aids. At the conference were a number of blind scientists and other blind professional people.

Almost all of them felt they would not make use of such aids if they were invented. As Dr. Schimmel writes: "These were individuals who had made their adjustment to blindness and objected to a mechanical solution to their problem."

Is this surprising? Perhaps we're not seeing it properly.

We make use of many devices to stretch our senses. Each, like ultrasound or X-rays, gives us a different view of things. And each view is only a partial view, for the world around us is rich enough so that whether we have four or five or fifty senses, they can show us only a part of it at a time. It is ideas and imagination that put the world together.

The inner world of each person's mind is the world of ideas and imagination. It is just as rich as the outside world from which its ideas come. But no "mechanical solutions" are going to make even a part of someone else's ideas visible to us. Only understanding can do that.

These blind professional men and women work just as efficiently as their sighted colleagues. They see them-

Using the Optacon, the girl can read ordinary print. The teacher moves the scanner over the letters. The scanner changes the letters into electrical signals. The girl feels these signals on her forefinger. Later, she learns to use the scanner by herself for reading. (*Malcolm E. Weiss*)

selves and the world very clearly. So do most blind children. But growing up in a sighted world, they do need help from the sighted. What they need most is for us to see them.

SOURCES FOR QUOTED MATERIAL

Hartman, David. As quoted in Asbell, Bernard. "A Farsighted School and a Sightless Student Are Making History." *Today's Health*, October 1974.

Hertz, Heinrich. "Über Strahlen elektrischer Kraft (On Rays of Electrical Force). *Annalen der Physik*, 1887. Translated by W. F. Magie in *A Source Book of Physics*, New York, 1935. As quoted in Wightman, William P. D. *The Growth of Scientific Ideas*. New Haven: Yale University Press, 1953.

Schimmel, Herbert. "Visual Prosthesis: Is It Feasible? Will It Be Useful?" Lowell Institute Lectures in Medicine, Massachusetts Eye and Ear Infirmary, February 6, 1973.

Skorokhodova, Olga. *How I Perceive, Imagine and Understand the World Around Me*. Moscow, 1972. As quoted in "The World Around Me," *The UNESCO Courier*, March 1974.

Sorter, Judi. "Blindness Seen Through Reactions." *The Blind Digest*, May 1968. As quoted in Monbeck, Michael E. *The Meaning of Blindness, Attitudes Toward Blindness and Blind People*. Bloomington, Indiana: Indiana University Press, 1973.

Weiss, Carl. "Reality Aspects of Blindness as They Affect Case Work." *The Family*, February 1946.

INDEX